LONDON

CITY ON A RIVER

April 2000
London Trip
Margaret & John Penney

DAVID PATERSON

JULIAN CRITCHLEY

PEAK PUBLISHING LTD

© Peak Publishing Ltd., 1997
© Introduction: Julian Critchley, 1997
© Photographs & additional text: David Paterson, 1997
None of the photographs has appeared previously
in any other book and none has been computer-
enhanced or altered in any way.

First published in Great Britain by:
Peak Publishing Ltd.,
88 Cavendish Road,
London SW12 0DF.

ISBN 0 9521908 3 4
Cataloguing in British Library publication data applied for.

Paterson, David
London - City On A River
1. London
2. Photography
3. Travel

For Mayumi and Sean.

Other titles in series with this volume:
The Cape Wrath Trail – A 200-Mile Walk Through the North-West Scottish Highlands (ISBN 0 9521908 1 8)
Heart of the Himalaya – Travels in Deepest Nepal (ISBN 0 9521908 2 6)

Designed by Peak Publishing
Typeset in Opus 11/14
Originated & printed by:
C&C Offset Printing Co. Ltd., Hong Kong

CONTENTS

Tower Bridge in the early morning

The River Thames & Battersea Power Station

PREFACE

London is a city of almost overwhelming size and complexity but, since landscape is what interests me most as a photographer, it was the skylines and panoramas of the city which first claimed my attention when I came with my family to live here nearly fifteen years ago, and they fascinate me still.

Though it is not a beautiful city, London has many beautiful buildings. It was the hub of a once-great empire, with all of the palaces and pomp which that implies, and it is still – after all that has happened – *the* royal city. London is one of the great financial capitals of the world, with high-tech temples to the great god Money rising in canyons of marble and glass, and it is a cultural centre whose art galleries, orchestras and opera houses, theatres and museums draw visitors from all around the globe. It is an important seat of learning, with universities, colleges, institutes, think-tanks and teaching hospitals, and it is the cosmopolitan melting-pot for all the peoples and races of the world.

But everyone who knows the city has their own version of London – perhaps just their own locality, or some particular area, or aspect of its culture or atmosphere, which to them to defines the city. To me, what gives London its unique character is its river, the Thames.

From the still-futuristic Thames Barrier in the east to Hampton Court Palace twenty miles or so upriver, all the great monuments both old and new – the icons of the city – lie on the riverbanks or within a stone's-throw of them: Canary Wharf, Greenwich, the Tower of London, Tower Bridge, the City, St Paul's, Royal Festival Hall, Lambeth Palace, Westminster, the Tate Gallery, Battersea Power Station, Hampton Court; and those are just the first which spring to mind; there are many others.

As the mid-'90s passed and my deadlines edged ever closer, I longed for a few days of deep snow to cloak and change the city, but London was enjoying a sequence of mild winters, and it never happened. Only in the parks could I try to use the photographs to hint at any seasonal changes. Winter and summer alike, however, many of the buildings I wanted to photograph disappeared under scaffolding and tarpaulin, to remain that way for months; sometimes for years. At the time of writing, the dome of St Paul's has been wrapped in dirty tarpaulin for as long as I care to remember; Big Ben is held hostage behind a barrier of tower-cranes, and much of Parliament Square has become a permanent building-site. The City of London simply *is* a construction site; the tearing down and re-building never stops, day or night.

So I prowled the river, early and late, and if the book contains more photographs along its banks than seems reasonable, I can't really apologise. At five o'clock on a mid-summer morning there is more life on the river than in the streets; and on a still evening when sunset light floods along the Thames, London *is* beautiful, almost. The traffic-noise muffled and far away, the calm flow of the river, open skies overhead and the chance to let the eyes rest, for once, on a horizon – I went back to these time and time again, and still do.   D. Paterson

The Royal Chelsea Hospital

Introduction:
A Reminiscence by Julian Critchley

I was born on December 8, 1930 in the main maternity ward of the Great Northern Hospital. This has no significance whatever, save that it encouraged my mother who was a Shropshire girl, to claim that, having been born in the sound of Bow Bells, I was therefore a cockney. I have never regarded myself as a cockney, although I have lived for most of my life in or near London, and only in my sixties have retired to Ludlow in Shropshire. My father was born in Bristol in 1900, and was a brilliant medical student at the City's university, but decided to become a big fish in a big pond and moved to London to practise neurology. He had no wish to stay in the much smaller pond that was Bristol, where we might have lived in a fine house in Clifton, over-looking the suspension bridge. My mother, who was a nurse and mid-wife, married the cleverest doctor on the ward, and abandoned Shropshire and the maternal cottage for the life of the wife of a prosperous London-based neurologist. I was her first child.

At the time of my birth my parents rented a flat in Chelsea before that part of London became quite as fashionable as it is today. The King's Road was quite arty, and the painter Augustus John was a neighbour, but my first real recollection is of our flat in Barnes, south of the river and adjacent to the Southern Railway Bridge that crosses the Thames. This meant an annual party for the Oxford and Cambridge boat-race, the best-attended free sporting spectacle in the world, which is held in March. The crews pulled past our roof garden, and I was a supporter of the light blues, although for no good reason. Later, I was to go to Oxford.

The significance of my father renting flats in Chelsea and Barnes was their comparative cheapness. Rented accommodation was much easier to come by in the years between the wars, and bank managers were very reluctant to lend money for house purchase. Indeed, in 1939, when my father was neurological consultant to several major London teaching hospitals, and drove a new Daimler, his bank manager refused him a loan of £1000 which would have enabled him to buy the house we then occupied in Swiss Cottage.

Barnes is a pretty inner London suburb, late Victorian in flavour, which has now become a fashionable place for media people to live. It has more than its share of good "restaurants de quartier." (The BBC television studios are just a twenty minute drive across the river, and the broadcaster Peter Snow, for example, lives in a pretty, terraced house in Barnes. We dined with him in the '80s, and his dining-room was served by his electric train-set which brought the food to the table.) But I remember very little of Barnes, save the boat race and falling out of father's Lea Francis on to the road. I was sent to the Frobel School for Infants, which at that time was well in advance of standard educational practice, and was conveniently situated in neighbouring Roehampton. I was not to be so fortunate later on.

South of the river has always been less fashionable than the north, just as the west of London is smarter when compared to the East End. Some areas of the south had, and still have, a certain cachet: Barnes, Richmond, Clapham Common, Blackheath, Dulwich and parts of Greenwich, but by and large it consists of an enormous working-class area in which high-rise flats have largely replaced the old artisans' cottages. The smarter areas often lie on the higher ground from which there are splendid views across London to the distant northern heights of Hampstead and John Betjeman's Highgate.

London has four typical styles of architecture: Georgian, both early and late; High Victorian red; post-war brutalist flats clustered on estates, and a remnant of 19th century cottages which made up the bulk of pre-war housing in the East End, so much of which was demolished by Hitler's Luftwaffe in the blitzes of 1940/41.

The city is like Paris in that it consists of a collection of villages, some of which still retain their identity. There has been, since the war, a slow process of gentrification which has changed the nature of parts of central London like Islington (where Tony Blair had his home), North Kensington and West Hampstead. These are areas, once smart, which had declined in the early years of this century, only to recover as greater prosperity – and the proximity of the City of London – made their run-down Georgian houses cheap and desirable. As many working-class Londoners were "decanted", to use the awful jargon word, to places out in Essex and close to where Heathrow Airport now lies, the marginal areas became smarter as young professional couples, with two jobs and a flair for interior decoration, re-occupied what had been working class dwellings.

But I should return to my own experience of London. In 1935, we moved from Barnes to No. 4 Harben Road, NW6. Once again the house was rented. It no longer exists, having been pulled down by the Hampstead Borough Council in the late fifties to make way for council flats. But many such houses remain and are typical of the less smart areas of Hampstead, West Hampstead, Belsize Park and the Irish quarter, Kilburn. No. 4 was tall and narrow, three floors and a kitchen basement, covered in a pale grey stucco. In the front a long flight of steps leading from a small garden with two acacia trees; in the back a larger walled garden with two not very flourishing pear trees. Harben Road was a middle-middle-class street, where every house had a living-in servant (we had two, my cousin Daisy who was my nanny, and Laura, the maid). The house had three principal rooms, three main bedrooms and two attics. The basement consisted of the kitchen, sitting-room and larder and pantry. We had a fridge and coal-house. The house had been built during the 1860's, and fronted the main LMS Euston to Glasgow railway-line over which ran the old Great Central from Marylebone to Sheffield. We were built on higher ground, and the railways ran out of sight but not completely out of sound.

No. 4 was in the postal district known as NW6, but only just. The much smarter NW8 was to the south, a district known as St John's Wood where rich adulterers had built pretty early 19th century villas for their amorata. St John's Wood bordered on Regent's Park, London's prettiest. To the north of Swiss Cottage was the even grander NW3, which included Hampstead Village, so smart that it was not served by the ubiquitous red buses, but instead by a deeply buried Northern Line tube train. A trip from Harben Road to Hampstead Heath meant a long drag on foot up Fitzjohn's Avenue, flanked by large late Victorian mansions, some of which had already been turned into nursing homes. My mother was sufficiently ashamed of "NW6" that she was often tempted to put "NW8" upon her letters.

When we returned from the war (my father had joined the Royal Navy and we had lived at the RN Hospital, Barrow Gurney, near Bristol) we found Swiss Cottage, and indeed the whole of London, battered and shabby. Everywhere, and in particular in the City, were bomb sites on which in summer flourished a purple weed. I was 14, and in the long holidays from Shrewsbury School, set about the exploration of London.

I had no friends in London. I would amuse myself by taking the tube train from Swiss Cottage to Harrow and back, travelling on the cheapest of tickets. At Finchley Road station the tube surfaced, and the route to Harrow, some ten miles distant, became a race track between the old Metropolitan railway pulled by ancient brown electric locomotives with names like "Alice", and what had been Great Central (by that time British Railways) express trains which were steam-hauled. I was a trainspotter before the title became pejorative.

The alternative to the train was the buses. The number 31 bus ran from Camden Town, directly southwards through the different "villages" of west London, driving through them with the zeal of a sociologist cutting into a layer cake. Kilburn was largely Irish; parts of North Kensington were as poor and ugly as the south of that Royal Borough was rich and beautiful. The 31 ended at World's End in Chelsea, which was to become by the sixties, King's Road and "swinging London".

The buses were cheap (lowest fare was a penny and a half in the old currency), the conductors matey as only cockneys can be, and it was a great pleasure to climb the pitching stairs to the top of the double-decker and sit on the front seat. I discovered the immensity of what was London by looking at the destination boards of buses. They could be headed for such unusual and unvisited places as Stoke Newington, Charlton, and Catford, or, if one were more daring, the Greenline buses would take one out of London to distant places like Gerrard's Cross, Guildford, or Erith and Crayford. The traffic in the late forties was much lighter, and the buses floated between unknown suburbs like so many flamingo-coloured birds. They were slower than the noisy tubes, but at least one could see where one was going.

In 1954, when I was up at Oxford wasting my time, my parents were obliged to move once again. This time my father rented an ugly flat in Bristol House, Southampton Row, Bloomsbury. He did so because it was within easy walking distance of the National Hospital of which he was Dean. Bloomsbury had, and still has, a certain glamour. It was very much the literary quarter, and the University of London with its tall, pre-war, modernist tower (the top floors were never used as no fireman's ladder could reach them), and the British Museum were "round the corner". There were long streets of Georgian houses, and at the bottom of Southampton Row, the

Chiswick landing-stage, from the Barnes shore of the Thames

Aldwych which had been built in the early years of the century, demolishing what were some of London's worst slums. At the Aldwych the trams (which did not finally disappear in London until the end of the '50s), vanished underground in a tunnel of their own, only to reappear suddenly on Waterloo Bridge.

On Sunday afternoons I would drive my Vespa scooter, or later my Model Y Ford, around the streets of the deserted City of London. The City is a city within a city, with its own police force and Lord Mayor. It was the world's leading financial centre, a position which may now have been taken over by Frankfurt. The poet T S Eliot wrote of the thousands who thronged the bridges leading into the City every weekday morning: *"Unreal City/Under the brown fog of a winter's dawn/A crowd flowed over London Bridge, so many/I had not thought death had undone so many..."*

Even today the City is under guard from the outrages of Irish terrorists, and the traffic moves ever more slowly. On weekdays it is packed with smart young employees of Merril Lynch, living bonus to bonus, and the great regiments of office workers who come to man the City's desks and computer-screens.

The Thames is London's river. I have often taken a river boat from Westminster Pier, and travelled down the river to Greenwich. What has happened during my lifetime is the gradual rebuilding of the south bank river frontage, which has always been by far the less distinguished of the two banks. Before the war, the cathedral architect Giles Gilbert Scott built Battersea Power Station, next to Battersea Gardens on the south bank. Although it is now but a shell its four enormous chimneys still stand,

and the building is "listed," that is, protected. Its future is uncertain, but lottery money might bring about its restoration. It featured in the film of Richard III which starred Ian McKellen, and which was set, incongruously but brilliantly, in the "fascist thirties".

The Festival of Britain, Herbert Morrison's pipedream, designed to celebrate the revival of Britain from the worst effects of the war and of Labour's post-war austerity, was responsible for the Festival Hall, although the Millenium Dome, begun on waste ground further down-river near Greenwich, now seems unlikely to go the same way as the Dome of Discovery, plans for which were abandoned. But the south bank has been steadily re-built and is protected by HMS Belfast, a Second World War cruiser, which is anchored off Tower Bridge.

The river boat takes one as far as Greenwich where the China clipper The Cutty Sark is berthed. It is still a great place to eat whitebait in pubs. The Royal Navy has left Greenwich, but the great complex of 17th and 18th century buildings, over-looked by the Queen's House and the Royal Observatory, remains London most distinguished architecture. Greenwich Park is fringed by Georgian houses of quality, and the roads lead inland to Blackheath where I lived with my first wife in the late fifties. The view from the hill on which the Observatory stands embraces half of London. It ranges over the City of London, and to the north and east where the old East End (now largely and badly rebuilt) shades into the flat, dull lands of Essex. But the new Dockland complex, built in the eighties and still not complete, dominates the skyline with Europe's tallest building.

From the early 18th century, London seen looking

northwards from Westminster or Waterloo Bridge, presented what was possibly the finest townscape in the world. It was painted by both Turner and Caneletto at a time when the city was dominated by St Paul's Cathedral which rose above every other building in sight. The northern bank of the river was lined by Whitehall Palace and the Savoy Palace, while the river itself, now largely neglected, was a busy thoroughfare. Today, the picture has almost completely changed. The dome of St Paul's that survived the fires of the blitz, no longer sets the scene. It has to be looked for, as do the spires of the many superb Wren churches in the City. Today the skyscrapers of the City of London, symbols of profit and prosperity (and no little peculation) jostle each other for pre-eminence. London could just as well be Houston, Texas, or Atlanta, Georgia, and we have allowed our architects and speculative builders to foul our nest.

The smartest parts of central London are the southern half of the Royal Borough of Kensington, including Camden Hill, Chelsea, parts of Westminster, Belgravia, Regent's Park, St John's Wood, and, of course, Mayfair which is bounded by Park Lane, Oxford Street (which is tatty and to be avoided), Bond Street and Piccadilly.

Like most large cities, London changes its character with a rapidity which can be quite bewildering. The cockney accent is uncommon in the parts I have listed, as these districts are the home of Sloane Rangers and elderly females who drop the "g" in "ing". They go huntin' at Harrods. However if it's cockney you are after, go to Stepney or Stratford; if its "Sarf London", a subtle variant of cockney found south of the river, then you should take a bus to the Elephant. Bengali has already replaced Yiddish throughout most of the old East End. Brixton, in south London, is the West Indian quarter.

London is an ever-changing city. Edgware Road was once the smart Jewish quarter of London; it is now, ironically enough, almost entirely Arab in character. Jews, who left Tsarist Russia at the turn of the century, first lived in poverty in the East End; as they became more prosperous they moved to Stamford Hill and Stoke Newington in North London; more prosperous yet and they moved to Golder's Green; while the very rich lived on or near the Edgware Road. The restaurants that were once kosher have become Lebanese, and the silent women hide their faces from the gaze of the infidel.

When I was first married in the fifties, my wife and I found a small flat in a large Georgian house in Blackheath, in south-east London. (Blackheath Village is one of the oases at which the middle classes stop to water in the wasteland of South London.) The buses came down the Old Kent Road which had once seen better days, past the Marquis of Granby, the boxers' pub, and the displays of second-hand cars that masked the frontages of what had been once merchants' houses, turning east towards New Cross, past the site of the Woolworth's on which the first V2 rocket fell in 1944, killing many hundreds. The authorities, fearful of panic among a war-weary population, talked of exploding gas-mains, but news of Hitler's second "terror weapon" could not long be hidden from the populace.

New Cross becomes Deptford, once the home of a Royal Dockyard, and then the road to Kent, obeying the rules which seem common to most cities, climbs steeply from Greenwich up to Blackheath Common, where the air is healthier. Blackheath itself is a large open common in the south-east of London, fringed by fine Georgian houses, the most spectacular of which is the Paragon, on the common's south side – ten large houses built in the mid-18th century, connected by colonnades.

The main disadvantage of Blackheath was its distance from either the West End or the City. Buses took too long, and I was forced to brave the rush hour and drive into London (where it was still possible to park during the day; meters were to come later.) The alternative was to use the Southern Railway that ran its electric trains from the outer suburbs of London into Victoria, Blackfriars, Charing Cross and Waterloo stations. The trains were frequent and fast, but were crowded so tightly that not everyone found a seat.

I was first elected to the House of Commons as a Conservative MP when we were living in Blackheath. I represented Rochester, some twenty miles down the road into Kent. Later, when I had remarried, I lost my seat, and we lived for a time in Chepstow Villas, near Nottinghill Gate. Notting Hill is a typical London crossroads, with areas of elegance such as Campden Hill, Kensington Church Street, and Notting Hill itself, abutting on what were then some of the worst slums of London, in North Kensington. The carnival, which is held in August every year, turns the whole area into a cacophony of West Indian music, and drives the respectable citizens to their country retreats.

London is famous for Big Ben and the Houses of Parliament, double-decker buses, now of different colours since the break up of London Transport, Buckingham Palace, the daily Changing of the Guard, and the black London taxicab with its tight lock and irascible drivers. There is little love lost between them and their rivals in the mini-cabs. The black taxis are, as often than not, Jewish owned and driven, and the driver who forces his views upon you, or plays his radio without your permission, is a daily hazard. But unlike the mini-cabs, proper taxi drivers are controlled, numbered and licensed, and are obliged "to take the knowledge", an exhaustive test of the streets of the capital carried out on motor bikes. London taxis are metered and the cost is clear, although tipping is regarded as obligatory whether or not the driver gets out of his seat to help elderly ladies with their luggage.

The shops, restaurants and hotels of London are among the best of the world, and prices are not as high as several other European capitals, for example Paris, Copenhagen and Stockholm. Harrod's, the large Knightsbridge store which boasts a "by appointment" to the Royal Family, is world-renowned. St James's is famous for Lobb's the hat-maker, and Berry Bros and Rudd, the wine-merchants, as well as for the "Economist" and the Carlton Club which is reserved solely for members of the Conservative party. Fortnum and Mason's in Piccadilly is London's best food store.

The real revolution that has taken place in London since I returned to live there in 1946, is the vast improvement in the quality of its food. In the past only the great hotels like the Ritz, the Dorchester or Claridges had famous restaurants of an international, that is to say, French standard. Today, one can eat better in London than in Paris, and for a good deal less. Elizabeth David, the food writer, started the trend in the years immediately after the end of the war and the end of food rationing, a trend that has culminated in making celebrities out of cooks, or rather "chefs". The Roux Brothers (Le Gavroche in Mayfair), Mossiman of the club of the same name, Pierre Marco White, Prue Leith, Gary Rhodes and the River Club are just a handful of celebrated people and places where it is necessary to book. At the same time as English, or Anglo/ French, cooking has improved beyond measure, there has been a burgeoning of ethnic restaurants, mainly Chinese or Indian (Bengali, in most cases), where it is possible to eat cheaply and well. In 1946, when I was discovering London there were just three proper Chinese restaurants, one in Shaftesbury Avenue called the Hong Kong, and two others, the Old Friends and the New Friends, down in Limehouse, then a shady run–down dockland quarter where the respectable took care to visit in fours. The docks have gone, but the two "Friends" remain. Now there is Chinatown, and the number of Chinese restaurants (mainly Cantonese) is legion.

The most colourful part of central London is Soho, once the Italian quarter, with Italian food shops and restaurants. Since the war it has gone through several phases. It has always been the haunt of gourmets, criminals and tarts, but for a time the strip shows and dirty book shops took over, the tatty Georgian houses sporting an array of door–bells opposite which would be the legend "Strict disciplinarian" or "French lessons given". More recently, the "sleaze" has been done away with and Soho has returned to being the haunt of good restaurants, art galleries, food shops, jazz clubs, all-night drinking dens, and the writer, the late Jeffrey Barnard.

While I was an MP, I was a privileged Londoner. Underneath Westminster there is a large, free, car park, and in a city where it is now almost impossible to park, that was luxury indeed. My place of work was guarded by a hand-picked force of elderly policemen, and my small office looked out directly from the first floor of "the Palace" on to Big Ben. I would be deafened by the striking of the world's most famous clock. My London Allowance permitted me to rent a room with my brother who lived between the Fulham and King's Roads or with my daughter, Susannah, who had a small flat in the outer suburb of Catford. There could have been no greater contrast between two areas of London: Chelsea, smart and exclusive, and Catford, a relatively poor patch of south London with a very cosmopolitan population.

Once inside the Houses of Parliament, which are, in fact, a Royal Palace (although the Queen is only permitted to set foot in one half of it) MPs can take pleasure in the Terrace which runs the full length of the river frontage of Barry's mid-Victorian masterpiece. The Terrace is a magnet in the summer months for tourists in river–boats which anchor before it, the guide giving a running commentary on the history, the architecture, and the idleness of MPs who can be seen drinking and eating long into a summer's evening.

When I was eight, I was evacuated to the wilds of Shropshire by my parents, to escape the attentions of the Luftwaffe, and I can remember being moved by a Noel Coward song called "The London I Love". Today I live in Ludlow, and pay London just the occasional visit. I may no longer "love" London quite so much, but who can help admiring its diversity and its magnificence?

Dawn over London from Parliament Hill, Hampstead.

The Pond, Blackheath Common

Tower Bridge, looking north

EASTERN APPROACHES

Few people, now, get their first sight of London from the Thames, but it is not long since London was a major port, the river bustling with shipping from around the world and the quays so busy that vessels had to wait for days or even weeks to unload. Today all that is gone, the docks filled in and built over, surrounded by office blocks, or turned into ponds for aquatic sports. A few small coastal vessels struggle up the river as far as Rotherhithe, and barges still carry building materials and heavy waste of all kinds up and down the river, but all the vitality, romance and mystery of a great seaport has disappeared, in London's case via the very unromantic modern container–port of Tilbury, a few miles nearer the sea. The names remain – West India Dock, Greenland Dock, Canada Dock – but all they do is tease us by stirring some vague nostalgia for times we never knew, when foreign travel meant more than catching the tube out to Heathrow Airport and being processed, like peas, into whichever flying tin-can is taking us onwards.

The first great artefact you would see if approaching by river from the east is the Dartford Bridge, but as it lies beyond the Greater London boundary it is also outside the scope of this book. The next and more remarkable construction you would see is the Thames Barrier, its gleaming stainless–steel–covered domes reminiscent of Sydney Opera House (or a squadron of submarines from another planet). It was opened in 1984 and its ten great gates, which can pivot into position two metres above the highest recorded flood levels, guard London against that combination of high tides, high river levels and strong north–easterly gales which have periodically inundated parts of the city. The last time was in 1953, and prompted immediate planning for the Barrier.

A short distance upriver is Greenwich, which draws great crowds especially at weekends, but is best seen from quiet little Island Gardens across the river on the Isle of Dogs – not really an island but a narrow spit of land created by the tight meanders of the Thames, and reached from Greenwich by a recently–refurbished pedestrian tunnel. Not far away on the north bank of the river and visible from miles in any direction, Canada Tower is the new icon of London's East End, and a tourist attraction in its own right. It is also London's most visible public symbol of the 1980s, that decade of unrestrained development and corporate greed, and few people shed many tears when the Canary Wharf project ran into financial problems in the early 1990s. But it is a striking building and provides a focus where once London began its long slide into the flatlands of Kent and Essex.

Upriver from the splendid Georgian architecture of Greenwich there is little to relieve the mainly industrial reaches of the river east and west of Rotherhithe until Tower Bridge hoves in view, with the Design Museum and the smart row of converted Victorian warehouses along Butler's Wharf on the southern shore, where city money has conjured dereliction into fashionable flats.

The Thames Barrier

Five views of Canada Tower, Canary Wharf

Greenwich from Island Gardens

Greenwich Naval College

The Design Museum, Butler's Wharf

Looking east from Tower Bridge

The Thames at Butler's Wharf

Tower Bridge and the City of London

Tower Bridge at sun-up

Greenwich Naval College & The Isle of Dogs

This City now doth, like a garment, wear
The Beauty of the morning; silent, bare,
Ships, towers, domes, theatres and temples lie
Open unto the fields, and to the sky.

W. Wordsworth "Upon Westminster Bridge"

(London) is a monstrous ant–hill on the
plain of a too-busy World.

W. Wordsworth   "The Prelude", Book VII

St Paul's Cathedral, from the north-east

St Paul's & The City

The history of the consecrated site where St Paul's stands is at least as old as London itself, since a Roman temple was situated there and the first cathedral, a wooden structure dedicated to St Paul, was erected around 604. The next few hundred years saw a repeated tale of repeated burnings and destruction – by Vikings in 961 – until work on the first Norman cathedral was begun in 1087. This was a gigantic construction, longer and higher than the present building, with a towering spire which was struck and destroyed by lightning in 1447 and not restored for more than fifteen years.

The 16th and 17th centuries were the low point in the cathedral's history. The nave and other areas were used for trade – the sale of beer, fish, meat, vegetables and fruit; and servants, prostitutes, and (worse!) lawyers were available for hire. The first public lottery was held there, and brawls and even murder were not unknown. It was used as a stable and barracks by Cromwell's troops, and eventually much of the roof collapsed. In 1666 it was finally destroyed in the Great Fire of London.

Rebuilding under Sir Christopher Wren started in 1675, and for the next thirty-five years Wren and his master–builder, Thomas Strong, super–intended every detail of construction. This was remarkable enough, but in the same period Wren was also involved in the building of at least fifty fine churches around London.

The famous dome, known throughout the world, is actually a triple structure – the inner dome of decorated brick hides a cone of brick which supports the weight of the lantern, ball and cross. These top the outer dome, built of wood sheathed with lead. The cross is 365 feet (110m) above the pavement. Wren himself was one of the first people to be buried in the Cathedral's crypt, his grave marked by a plain slab of black marble.

St Paul's stands near the south–west edge of the City of London, now the financial quarter, but originally the site of the Roman settlement and later fortified medieval city whose walls stood until the late 18th century, and whose gates are remembered in present–day street names such as Bishopsgate and Aldgate. Within the City, as well as modern high-rise offices there are many fine examples of 18th and 19th century architecture – the headquarters of the trades, guilds and institutions which flourished with England's growing empire – but few from earlier years. The Fire of London destroyed not only St Paul's but also many fine Tudor buildings and thousands of the teeming and insanitary slums in which had festered the other scourge of London, the Plague. In the years following the Fire a new city was built on the street-plan of the old, this time in stone, and by the finest architects of the day including Wren – a phoenix rising from its ashes.

The north–east corner of the City is marked by the Tower of London, built in the 11th century as a fortress and prison, then the tallest building in London. Today it is overlooked by most other buildings in the vicinity including its neighbour, Tower Bridge, completed in1894.

Sunrise behind St Paul's, from Waterloo Bridge

Detail, the dome of St Paul's Cathedral

St Paul's & the City of London

City skyscrapers north of Leadenhall Street

The old Lloyds Building

The Lloyds Building

The City of London from The Monument

The Royal Exchange, City of London

St Bride's Church, Fleet Street

The NatWest Tower

Hay's Wharf and the London Bridge Building

The Thames, looking west from London Bridge

Finsbury Square, City of London

Tower Bridge & the Tower of London

The Bank of England, in evening light

Oh, London is a fine town,
A very famous city, Where all the streets are
paved with gold,
And all the maidens pretty.

George Coleman   "The Heir at Law"

I would sell London if I could find
a suitable purchaser.

King Richard I – raising funds for the
third crusade.

Dusk on the Thames at Westminster

Westminster Abbey

Oh, London is a fine town,
A very famous city, Where all the streets are
paved with gold,
And all the maidens pretty.

George Coleman   "The Heir at Law"

I would sell London if I could find
a suitable purchaser.

King Richard I – raising funds for the
third crusade.

King Richard, Lionheart, Palace of Westminster

PALACES & POWER

For a new visitor to London, the Palace and Abbey of Westminster and the surrounding area must be the most glamorous in the city. For a resident or habitue it is hard to appreciate the first impact of these great edifices; they are too familiar to us. Though visitors have always flocked in their thousands to these precincts, it is also hard to remember that only a few years ago the buildings were so soot-blackened that it seemed their natural state. Today, after years of cleaning, they are transformed and glow like amber in evening sunshine.

There has been a palace here since the days of Edward the Confessor, whose new residence on the north bank of the Thames was completed shortly before his death in 1066. The only part of the original building which has survived intact is Westminster Hall, built in 1097, whose magnificent hammer-beam roof was added in the 14th century by Rufus, son of William the Conqueror.

Most of the palace was destroyed by fire in 1834, only the Hall and the Jewel Tower (built in 1366) surviving. The architect Charles Barry was commissioned to carry out the re-building, assisted by the Gothic revivalist Augustus Pugin, who fitted out the new interiors with panelled ceilings, stained-glass, fireplaces, clocks, and wallpaper. Work was begun in 1837 and finished in 1860. The new clock-tower had a design height of 320 feet (95m), but it was discovered that the maximum height to which the massive mechanism could be raised was 150 feet, the height of Big Ben today. The clock had a chequered history, with changes of designer and manufacturer before it was even installed. Cracks were discovered in the bell which had to be re-cast; and the metal hands were so heavy that the clockwork could not raise them past the horizontal. St Stephen's Tower, in which the clock is housed, was damaged by bombs in 1941, along with much of the palace.

Just five minutes' walk from Westminster is St James's Palace, which is still occupied by members of the royal household. Buckingham Palace, the head-quarters of the monarchy since Queen Victoria's time, is just a few minutes further away.

Across the river, County Hall was for many years a symbolic, and at times real, adversary to the power of Westminster. Until centralised local government in London was abolished in 1986 it was the home of the Greater London Council, a Labour-dominated body, frequently at odds with Conservative governments. County Hall has been empty since 1986, and though there were plans to turn it into a hotel, there may yet be a city-wide authority re-established there.

Close by, Lambeth Palace has been the London headquarters of the Archbishop of Canterbury, head of the Church of England, since medieval times. Some small fragments of the buildings date from the 13th century, and the Tudor gatehouse of vivid red brick, built in 1485, is one of the most charming and well-known monuments anywhere on the south bank of the Thames.

Dusk on the Thames at Westminster

Westminster Abbey

St John's Church, Smith Square, Westminster

Buckingham Palace

The Palace of Westminster, in evening light

The Palace of Westminster

Lambeth Palace, seen across the Thames

The Albert Embankment, from Lambeth Bridge

Big Ben, from the Mall

The Palace of Westminster, from the south embankment

Trafalgar Square, and the shadow of Nelson!

Early morning, Trafalgar Square

St Margaret's Church, Westminster

Westminster Cathedral

Admiralty Arch and the Old Admiralty Building

Trafalgar Square & the National Gallery

The Institute of Contemporary Arts, the Mall

Nelson on his column, Trafalgar Square

Bush House (BBC Foreign Service), The Aldwych

At length they all to Merry London come,
To Merry London, my most kindly nurse,
That gave to me this life's first native source.

Edmund Spenser   "Prothalamion"

When it's three o'clock in New York it's
still 1938 in London

Bette Midler – in an interview with The Times
in 1978

Rose Trellis, Kew Gardens

WAY OUT WEST

South of the river and west of County Hall the great monuments thin out, and even along the north shore landmarks become rarer. The new MI6 headquarters, beside Vauxhall Bridge, is hardly great architecture (nor is Vauxhall Tower opposite, though it is extremely visible) but the long row of medium–rise 1960s office buildings which line the Albert Embankment – the south bank between Westminster and Vauxhall – has a strange hint of the Shanghai Bund about it. The Tate Gallery has a fine facade, but surely the grandest building along this reach of the Thames must be Battersea Power Station.

Its status as a listed building unfortunately did little or nothing to protect it during the laissez–faire years of the 1980s, and, monumental still, it lies wide–open to the elements, its roof torn off, everything of interest or value stripped out and its "developers" no doubt waiting until it can be declared unsafe, to be torn down to make way for profitable riverside apartments or offices.

It is a landmark in every sense. Opened in 1937, it is one of the largest brick constructions in the world. Initially it had only two chimneys but was later doubled in size and output to give it the fine and powerful symmetry still so evident today in spite of all the depredations it has suffered. A very modern idea included in the original design was that of combined heat and power – popular with present–day power-station engineers – and it supplied central heating from its waste hot water to nearby Churchill Gardens, an estate housing over six thousand people. It has been closed since 1983.

Across the road, Battersea Park was one of the first public parks or gardens in London, and was constructed in an effort to clean up a notorious area of vice and crime. Today, as well as the traditional attractions of boating pond and spacious walks, it is home to a large Japanese pagoda built by a Zen sect in the mid–'80s, one of the more surprising sights of south London.

Battersea itself is one of several comfortable and prosperous localities which line the riverbanks as you proceed west, followed by Putney, Barnes, Richmond, Twickenham and Kingston, across from Chelsea, Fulham and Chiswick. Along this stretch the bridges themselves are the major landmarks, and it is only at Hampton Court that a really remarkable building is reached. The Palace, in spite of frequent changes, remains a jewel of Tudor architecture. It was begun in 1514 by Thomas Wolsey, later Cardinal and Lord Chancellor of England, and when he fell from favour it was appropriated by Henry VIII, the first of many monarchs to make Hampton Court their main residence. Jane Seymour died there after giving birth to Henry's only son; Elisabeth I lived there (having first been imprisoned there) and is reported as working in the gardens herself among exotic plants such as tobacco and potato brought from abroad by her sea-captains. William and Mary built the maze, based on Wolsey's original 'labyrinth', and Hampton Court only ceased to be a royal residence during Victoria's reign.

The Tate Gallery

MI6 Headquarters, Albert embankment

Battersea Power Station and the Grosvenor Railway Bridge

Battersea Power Station – coal-handling cranes

The birds are coming . . . .

. . . . two sunset views from Battersea Bridge

Richmond, from Richmond Bridge

Dawn in Richmond Park

Hampton Court Palace gardens

Hampton Court Palace

Hampton Court Palace from the Privy Garden

The Palm House, Kew Gardens

London is the epitome of our times,
and the Rome of today.

Ralph Waldo Emerson "English Traits"

Hell is a city much like London –
A populous and smoky city.

Percy Bysshe Shelley "Peter Bell the 3rd"

Walthamstow Greyhound–Racing Stadium

NORTH & SOUTH

Away from the riverbanks there are attractions in both halves of the city (on either side of the Thames) but looking at a map of Greater London what is most striking is the great number of parks and gardens which have survived into the last years of the 20th century, avoiding the incursions of development and acting as the green lungs of the city. Beginning with St James's behind Westminster, a continuous chain of parks more than two-and-a-half miles (4kms) in length stretches away westwards through Green Park, Hyde Park and finally Kensington Gardens. To the north lies Regent's Park, home of the London Zoological Society; Primrose Hill is popular for its views of the city, and crowning the hill above Hampstead, the Heath is a favourite playground of rollerbladers, day-dreamers, swimmers in its many ponds, walkers and courting couples. Lovers of art and music are catered for at the magnificent Robert Adam mansion of Kenwood at the north edge of the Heath, with its superb collection of old–master paintings, and outdoor concerts, complete with fireworks, in summer.

On the south-west side of the city, the inter–connecting Richmond Park and Wimbledon Common provide an area of nearly twelve square miles – as large as the whole of Fulham, Chelsea and Westminster – of wide open spaces, wooded parkland, rides, walks and golf courses, and though these two are much the largest, every southern borough boasts its own green space: Clapham, Wandsworth, Tooting, Streatham, Brockwell,

Dulwich, Peckham and dozens more. It is often said that London has more parks and gardens than any other city in the world, and it is easy to believe the claim.

London south of the Thames, having developed much later and in response to the city on the other bank, inevitably has less history and fewer great buildings as a result, but it's not all gardens and grass – though there is Wimbledon, of course, with its annual tennis-fest, The Oval, and Crystal Palace stadium. There are fine houses in Charlton (Jacobean) and Eltham (Tudor), a museum and art gallery in Dulwich, the Imperial War Museum near the Elephant and Castle, and a scattering of fine churches. What *has* developed in south London is a vivacious street-life mainly based on the large ethnic populations of areas like Brixton, Tooting and Streatham, with colourful markets, exotic restaurants and a fairly wild variety of bars, pubs and clubs.

London north of the Thames, however, has Piccadilly, Soho, Covent Garden, Regent Street, the bookshops in Charing Cross Road, electronic alley in the Tottenham Court Road, Harrod's, Selfridge's, Liberty's, most of the concert venues and theatres, all the opera houses, nearly all the important art–galleries and museums and, of course, all the really posh hotels and restaurants. These are before you get to Lord's Cricket Ground, the British Museum and Library, the zoo, Alexandra Palace and the delights of Highgate Cemetery (tidied–up nowadays). On the downside, however, it does also have Islington.

The Serpentine Gallery, Hyde Park

Spring blossom in Hyde Park

The Natural History Museum, South Kensington

Harrod's Department Store, by night

(Top) Marble Arch

Victory Arch, Hyde Park Corner

(Top) The British Museum

St Pancras Station

The Hoover Building, Western Avenue

Holy Trinity Church, Clapham Common

Russell Square, Bloomsbury, with the University Senate Building

Kenwood House, Hampstead Heath

Midsummer sunset over
Clapham Boating Pond

Piccadilly Circus by night

'I beg your pardon' said the Mole.
'You must think me very rude; but all this is
so new to me. So - this - is - a - River!'
'The River', corrected the Rat.

Kenneth Graham "The Wind in the
Willows"

And dream of London,
small and white and clean,
The clear Thames bordered,
by its gardens green.

William Morris   "The Wanderers"

The Thames from Riverside Walk, South Bank

RIVERSIDE

Many parts of central London could lay claim to being the heart of the city, but for a lover of the river the title can only go to that stretch of the Thames between Lambeth Bridge and Blackfriars, where the river swings north and east round a long curve which turns it through nearly ninety degrees, so that at Westminster the flow is almost due north, but at Blackfriars due east.

At virtually the geometric centre of the arc between these two points, Waterloo Bridge must still be the best viewpoint for all that London has to offer. The City and St Paul's lie along the eastern horizon, Big Ben and the turrets of the Palace of Westminster spike the skyline to the west. Between them, ranged along both banks of the river, lies the greatest concentration of all that goes to make a great capital city. The Courts of Justice, Temple and the Inns of Court, Somerset House, the Savoy Hotel, Shell Mex House, the new Charing Cross station complex, Whitehall and Westminster line the northern shore; opposite them, among others, stand the IPC and LWT towers – representing the modern media of magazine publishing and television – the Oxo building, the Hayward Gallery, National Theatre and Royal Festival Hall, St Thomas' Hospital, County Hall and Lambeth Palace. Out of sight but little distance away are Waterloo Station; Covent Garden; Trafalgar Square and the National Gallery; the Old Vic Theatre; the Strand and Fleet Street. All human life is there: rich and poor; art and entertainment; politics, religion and law; commerce and finance; broadcast media and publishing; the best of food, drink and gracious living.

The river has brought it all here – no longer in the literal sense, as a trading highway – but by being the reason for London's existence. Ever since the ancient inhabitants of a few mud and wattle huts on the north shore decided it might be a good idea to establish a crossing to their counterparts on the other side, the development of the city we know today, or something very like it, has probably been inevitable. When the Romans came, and made it their headquarters, that process was reinforced. Before long it was the largest town in England, and no other city ever really challenged it for supremacy. When the country was unified following the Norman conquest in the 11th century it became and has remained the seat of the monarch and capital city. By the end of the 18th century it was the largest and richest city in the world, sustained by the greatest empire the world had ever seen. It no longer has the empire, though it is still very wealthy. And it is still a great city.

The Thames has seen it all come and go. Today it flows impassively through its modern channel of concrete and stone as once it flowed past the empty water–meadows of pre–history. Though rivers are usually understood as symbols of change, if you lean on a parapet somewhere along the south bank and watch for a while as London is torn down and re-built around you, you just might begin to see the Thames as the most permanent thing around.

Blackfriars Bridge & the City of London . . . .

. . . . from Waterloo Bridge

Blackfriars Rail Bridge

The National Theatre, South Bank

Waterloo Station's new Eurostar terminus

Early morning on the south embankment

County Hall and the Shell Centre

The Gatehouse, Lambeth Palace

The Shell Centre, South Bank

The Sphinx, Victoria Embankment

St Paul's and the City of London,
from Waterloo Bridge

Looking west from Waterloo Bridge

The Thames & Shell Mex House, at dusk

Dusk over St Paul's Cathedral & the City of London

Thanks are due to all the friends and colleagues who gave encouragement and advice during the preparation of the book, especially Iain and Fiona Roy, who as ever prevented the publication of my many errors by their assiduous proof reading: also to my wife, Mayumi, who gave constant support, and never complained at being disturbed by my frequent dawn starts. When writing the short introductions to each section of the photography, I made frequent use of "The History of London" by W.R. Dalzell, the "Cadogan Guide to London" by A. Gumbel, and "The London Encyclopaedia" (ed. Weinreb & Hibbert) for dates, information and general fact–checking.   D. Paterson, Clapham, October '97

David Paterson (b. 1945) read chemistry at Edinburgh University and had a previous career as a chemical engineer before turning full-time to photography in 1971. He has since worked for major companies, magazines, advertising agencies and design clients around the world, and has been active in the world of publishing since the mid–1980's. In 1992 he founded Peak Publishing, dedicated to the production of high–quality illustrated books of his and other photographers' work. This is his eighth book, the others including English landscape, the Himalayas and his own special interest, the Scottish Highlands and Islands.

Julian Critchley was born in 1930, the son of the distinguished neurologist Dr Macdonald Critchley. He was educated at Shrewsbury School, the Sorbonne and Pembroke College, Oxford. He was elected Tory MP for Rochester in 1959, and for Aldershot in 1970. Owing to ill–health he retired from Parliament in May 1997. Critchley is a writer, broadcaster and journalist with thirteen books to his credit. His autobiography "A Bag of Boiled Sweets" (Faber) was published in 1995 and became a best-seller. He has also cooperated with David Paterson in "Borderlands", a book about the Welsh Marches. In 1995, he received a knighthood for public and political services.

The cover photograph shows the panorama of the Barbican, St Paul's Cathedral and the City of London, at dawn, from Waterloo Bridge.